Primroses and auriculas

Cover: a Barnhaven double polyanthus seedling (photograph by Hazel Blackburn)
Overleaf: 'Hew Dalrymple', a green-edged show auricula

Primroses and auriculas

A Wisley handbook

Brenda Hyatt

Cassell

The Royal Horticultural Society

Cassell Educational Limited
Artillery House, Artillery Row
London SW1P 1RT
for the Royal Horticultural Society

First published 1989

British Library Cataloguing in Publication Data

Hyatt, Brenda,
    Primroses and auriculas
    1. Gardens. Primulas. Cultivation
    I. Title II. Royal Horticultural Society
    III. Series
    635.9′33672

    ISBN 0-304-31658-X

Photographs by W. Stewart, Michael Warren,
P. Tallboys, Gwen Baker, A. Hawkes, Harry Smith
Collection, Hazel Blackburn, Jim Gill, John Garey
Line drawings by Rita Johnson
Design by Lesley Stewart
Phototypesetting by Chapterhouse, Formby
Printed in Hong Kong by Wing King Tong Co. Ltd

Contents

The primrose

Introduction

On first sight the primrose gives instant pleasure, its simple beauty assuring us that winter is finally losing its grip. Childhood memories may be stirred of primroses growing in woodland, along banks or under hedgerows and more noticeably in profusion on the hillsides. The primrose is one of the first of our native plants to bloom in spring, appearing quite unexpectedly, with its pale yellow flowers charming every passer-by.

It is quite common to see near-white primroses growing among the yellow. In the sixteenth century, these and other natural sports – the double white and double sulphur primroses – were very popular in gardens. Mutations in form such as the jack-in-the-green and hose-in-hose were also well known at that time. Most of these can still be enjoyed by present-day gardeners, together with the large number of modern hybrids which are now available in a constantly widening range of colours.

The close relative of the primrose, the polyanthus, has been equally common in gardens since the seventeenth century. Although at first it had only reddish-coloured flowers, numerous forms were developed, the most important being the gold-laced polyanthus. In the early nineteenth century, this became highly prized as a florists' flower, with skilled growers competing to "perfect" it. Today, polyanthus are available in almost every conceivable colour, proving their value, along with primroses, as garden plants.

Opposite: Country Cottage mixture, one of the Barnhaven primrose seed strains

Single primroses

The primrose, *Primula vulgaris*, is a native of Britain and Europe and has been cultivated, together with its various mutations, for several hundred years. However, it was only in the seventeenth century that coloured primroses appeared in gardens, thanks mainly to the introduction of the mauve-pink *P. vulgaris* subsp. *sibthorpii* from the Mediterranean region. After this, little further development of the single primrose took place, although there were a few named forms which were quite familiar to gardeners at the end of the nineteenth century. The great breakthrough came in 1912, with the arrival of *P. juliae* from the Caucasus. This primrose, with bright purple yellow-centred flowers, has become the parent of hundreds of hybrids, referred to collectively as Juliana primroses. They come in a wide variety of colours, some brilliant, others soft and subtle, and often have polyanthus-type flowers. Although many of the original Julianas have been lost, some have survived and are well worth seeking out, while new ones are always being added.

The jack-in-the-green, hose-in-hose and other deviations from the normal primrose were particularly sought after in Elizabethan times. The first carries its flowers sedately within a ruff of leaves and the second has one flower growing from the centre of another in a most unusual and attractive way. Again, they may be of either primrose or polyanthus habit. Both these curiosities were popular in gardens until about the 1830s, with many named forms, most of which have disappeared from cultivation. Nevertheless, they are still being grown and there has even been a double-flowered jack-in-the-green developed recently. Chance seedlings with abnormal flowers sometimes arise among ordinary primroses.

CULTIVATION

Situation and soil

Although primroses are capable of growing in a variety of situations and are by no means difficult, they are far happier and more robust in partial shade. An ideal position is where the early morning sun reaches them, or perhaps in dappled sunlight, both of which will encourage the blooms to appear over a longer period. The plants themselves will also be healthier if sheltered from strong sunshine. In smaller gardens the choice of situation may be

Primula 'Wanda' is the most widely grown of the Juliana hybrids

limited, but primroses can be planted between taller-growing plants, which will provide the necessary shading in the height of summer.

In their chosen environment of woodland clearings, primroses are naturally surrounded by continuous supplies of leafmould, which gives an indication of their basic needs. They thrive in a good rich loam and, in this type of soil, enriched periodically by incorporating well-decayed manure and peat, the roots will find all the necessary nourishment. Moistness about their roots is essential in spring and summer, but they should never become waterlogged, particularly during the winter months, when the dormant roots could rot and cause the complete loss of the plant. If the bed is slightly raised or sloped, it will ensure sufficient winter drainage.

Primroses thoroughly dislike being exposed to strong drying winds, which can ruin the foliage and put them under extreme stress. A low wall will shelter them from the bitter northeasterly blasts that can be so damaging. An alternative is to erect a small fence with some strong netting, which will considerably lessen the effect of the wind and protect the plants at the same time.

9

Planting

The ideal planting period for primroses is from early to late autumn. They will then have time to develop into sturdy plants before facing the winter frosts and to produce good flowers for the following spring. Occasionally, the roots may not become established and a heavy frost will effectively lift them out of the soil; in this case, the plants will need to be firmly replanted as soon as the soil is frost-free. Never attempt to plant them when the soil is frozen or caked dry.

The primrose should be planted deeply, for it develops fresh roots annually from the crown of the plant, which must have access to nourishment to develop their new crowns in turn. These new crowns tend to emerge above the soil level initially and soil or, preferably, a mulch should be pushed up closely against them, to feed them while they are preparing for independence from the old rootstock. The mulch, consisting of peat, well decayed manure and leafmould, will also be a safeguard against dryness. It emulates the natural conditions that primroses enjoy in their woodland habitat. New roots develop several weeks after the spring flowering period, usually during June and July, their main function being to restock the plant with the necessary energy and strength to help it withstand the coming winter. Meanwhile, the old rootstock becomes far less active and is of little use after a couple of years; it can be completely discarded when the plant is ready for splitting.

Primroses are best planted about 12 in. (30 cm) apart, which allows them to remain uncrowded, but they can be placed a little closer to heighten the effect of "carpet-bedding". The smaller-flowered kinds will look better if planted about 6 in. (15 cm) apart.

Splitting and dividing

It is advisable to split primroses before too many crowns develop around the old rootstock, otherwise they will flower less well. There is no set rule, but if a plant grows more than three crowns, I regard it as ready for splitting and replanting. The roots are particularly active in early spring and early autumn and it is best to divide the plants just prior to this, giving the small divisions plenty of time to become established before their growth once again naturally slows down. They will also have had the opportunity to develop deep roots, which will sustain them during the hot spells of summer and the unknown rigours of winter.

Never attempt to divide the plants when the soil is hard and dry, for it will be very difficult and the roots will inevitably be broken. Dividing the plants after a few showers, in naturally damp condi-

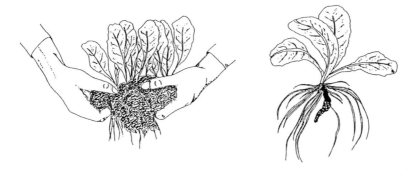

Figure 1: left, primrose ready for division; right, primrose after division – remove old lower rootstock before replanting

tions, is far easier and the results will be much more satisfactory. Dig out the complete plant and remove the soil with a small fork in a downward movement, until the crowns with their own roots are clear to see. Gently pull each crown away from the old rootstock, label as necessary and replant firmly into prepared soil or individual pots of enriched loam. Water them well and place the pots in a shady spot. In six to eight weeks a good root system will develop. However, the new roots are extremely vigorous and must not be allowed to become root-bound. They will adjust to their independence very quickly when transplanted into the prepared ground.

There are often small signs of growth left on the old rootstock and, if the form is rare or particularly precious to you, or perhaps stocks are low, it too can be replanted deeply in the open ground. The new shoots will become established crowns during the next 12 months and can then be separated as before. Any resultant wounds from this splitting should always be cleaned and dusted with sulphur dust, to protect the plants from rot or other disease, before replanting.

PROPAGATION

There are three main methods of propagating primroses – division (see above); layering; and seed. The only way to increase named forms is by the first two methods.

Layering

Layering is a useful method for propagating jack-in-the-green primroses, which are still uncommon. Their blooms, held quite

11

high and erect within a green leaf-like ruff, may be single, semi-double or fully double, but all will respond readily to layering. This should be carried out directly flowering has finished, while the ruff is still fresh and green. Spread moist peat around the base of the plant in preparation and collect a few wire clips together. Each stem bearing a single ruff is then gently bent down to the level of the soil, placed in an upright position and pressed lightly into the peat in the same way as strawberry runners are planted. Secure carefully but firmly, with the clips around the upper stem pushed just below soil level. The ruff remains exposed and within a few weeks a new plantlet will be noticed growing from inside the ruff. Leave it growing in this way until you are sure that it is strongly and independently rooted. It will then be sturdy enough to handle and may be severed from the parent plant, cutting the stem by which it has been attached. I usually leave the new plantlets until early autumn before transplanting them into their prepared bed.

Seed

It is not necessary to sow primrose seed immediately. To do so with fresh seed could coincide with hot dry spells, which are most unfavourable for good germination. The seed needs to be kept cool and airtight and can be stored in a screw-top jar in the refrigerator until you are ready to sow.

Winter sowing under glass: If you are on hand to check soil moisture, primrose seed can be sown from December to February in a

Figure 2: layering jack-in-the-green

Our native common primrose, *Primula vulgaris*

cold greenhouse or cold frame. Even at this time of year, it is important not to let the soil dry out. The soil will freeze and thaw throughout this period, which is perfectly normal, and the seed should start to germinate from March onwards.

Wild primrose seed does not need any glass protection and pans of freshly sown seed can stand outside throughout the winter months regardless of the weather, germinating from early spring onwards.

Spring sowing outdoors: If the seed is sown from March to May, the pans must be kept in a cool place outside. The seeds may show no sign of movement until they have felt the effects of frost, in which case germination can take many months. It is very import-ant to keep the compost moist at all times and to remember that primrose seed does not need heat to encourage germination. If the temperature rises above 65°F (18°C), the seeds may become subject to a condition called heat-induced dormancy and the majority of them will not germinate.

Sowing method: Peat-based seed compost is suitable for primrose seed and is readily available from garden centres and shops. Fill a seed pan to within approximately $\frac{1}{2}$ in. (1 cm) of the top and sow the seed thinly and evenly over the surface. Water in thoroughly and leave the pan to drain. Primrose seeds need maximum light to

Left: *Primula vulgaris* subsp. *sibthorpii* quickly forms a carpet of colour
Right: the unusual double-flowered jack-in-the-green

assist germination and must not be covered with compost. Simply cover the pan with fine netting, which will admit the necessary light and allow good air circulation. Watering through this is quite easy. If the pan is standing outside, the netting will also protect the seeds from heavy rain showers, which could dislodge them, and will shade them from lengthening periods of strong sunlight. *Never allow the compost to dry out.* It is far safer to give the pan a thorough watering when required, rather than frequent small amounts, which will only encourage the young seedlings to damp off at soil level. If there is any sign of seedlings dying from damping off, water the pan immediately with a benomyl solution at the recommended rate.

Seedlings do not appear simultaneously and it is better to leave the first ones to grow on a little, while waiting for most of the remainder to emerge. Removal of the first seedlings too quickly may dislodge and damage the rest. Keep a watchful eye on the early seedlings and do not let them grow higher than about 1 in. (2.5 cm), which would exclude light from the shorter seedlings. At this stage, the taller seedlings should be lifted out individually with utmost care and with as little soil disturbance as possible and transplanted into seed trays. Within a short period, the next batch will be ready for transplanting too. However, do not discard the seed pan for a few months, as smaller batches of seedlings often continue to appear intermittently.

Transplanting into seed trays or pots: Any proprietary potting compost can be used when transplanting primrose seedlings into seed trays or boxes or individual pots. I prefer a loam-based

14

compost, JI no. 2, and for every 2 gallon (9 litre) measure I add a quarter measure of well-rotted farmyard manure, mixing them together thoroughly. Choose a tray at least 4 in. (10 cm) deep, for the roots like to be kept as cool as possible, and fill it to within $\frac{1}{2}$ in. (1 cm) of the top with the compost mixture, which should be fairly moist. The seedlings may remain in the tray for three months or more and will need room to develop, so plant them evenly, leaving a gap of at least 2 in. (5 cm) around each. Gently firm them into the compost, water thoroughly and place the tray (or pots) in a cool shady spot outside.

The seedlings will not have to be disturbed again until they are planted out, but regular inspection, especially in hot weather, is essential. They require constant moisture and will become very distressed if allowed to dry out at any time. Spray the leaves with cold water when the surrounding atmosphere is particularly dry and they will feel much more comfortable. If a white mottling effect appears on the leaves during a hot dry spell, red spider mite is usually the cause. Increasing the regular spraying with cold water should discourage further attacks on the plants. Seedlings in pots will tend to dry out more quickly than those in trays or boxes and more attention to watering will be necessary.

Transplanting into open ground: It is obviously an advantage if seedlings can be transferred into the open ground as soon as they have established strong root systems in their trays or pots. This will give the roots ample space to develop, provided the ground is well prepared. Dig the soil thoroughly and deeply, adding plenty of humus – either peat or well-rotted animal manure, or a combination of both – and an inorganic fertilizer such as Growmore, scattering it evenly over the soil at 2 oz per sq. yd (70 g/m²). Well-rotted horse manure will help to lighten a heavy soil, while well-rotted cow manure will help to bind a light soil.

The seedlings should be planted firmly with their crowns on the surface. If possible, shade them for at least ten days with a layer of netting, for they can scorch very easily until they become sturdy and well established. Although preparation of the soil will improve moisture-retention around the roots, the plants will still need regular watering, particularly during very hot spells, either early in the morning or during the evening.

Seedlings which are left in trays until autumn before transplanting will have developed into larger plants, with much thicker roots and a more mature leaf growth. Outer leaves which are already past their best should be removed. If the roots are too long for the depth you have dug, cutting them back to about 4 in. (10 cm) in length will not hurt the plant, whereas bending the roots

15

to fit the available space will definitely be harmful. Plant each primrose firmly and maintain the necessary watering if there is a dry period. A rush of growth will be seen, including a few out of season blooms, but once the frosts start to become more intense, the plants will withdraw into themselves, biding their time during the days of shortened light and greater cold.

Fertilizers: The reawakening of the primroses in early spring will be governed by the gathering warmth and the increase of daylight hours. This is the time to decide which fertilizers to use and when. There is a wide range of fertilizers available, made up with varying proportions of the essential ingredients – nitrogen (N), phosphates (P) and potash (K). Numbers on the container label indicate the ratio of the contents. As the plants noticeably resume growth, a fertilizer high in nitrogen should be applied weekly for four to six weeks. This will promote leaf growth, which is important for the plant as the leaves are the means by which it digests and stores energy. Change to a fertilizer with a higher proportion of potash and phosphates when the new buds begin to emerge low within the centre of the plant. This will slow down leaf growth and promote the growth of the flowers. Continue this weekly feed until colour is seen in the buds and then stop feeding, for the fertilizer has now served its purpose.

It is helpful to understand the reasons for using these different fertilizers. Nitrogen, which encourages leaf growth, is safe to use in spring when the cells within the new soft growth are expanding. However, it should not be applied in autumn, because it will stimulate these developing cells, which would be unable to cope with a sudden frost. The tender new growth would freeze completely, resulting in the loss of the whole plant. Potash and phosphates promote the growth of flowers, but they can also be given if the autumn is particularly mild, when they will reduce the cell growth in the leaves and assist the plants to harden off in preparation for the winter. All primroses, not just seedlings, will benefit from the use of fertilizers.

GROWING IN POTS

Primroses are very popular as indoor pot plants and, when grown in this way, they not only prolong the flowering season but allow one to enjoy to the full the first glimpse of spring blooms. The little extra trouble is well worthwhile. As the winter begins to loosen its grip – early March in southern parts of the country and a week or two later further north – carefully lift a few chosen plants from the garden. The new leaves should be forming, showing that the

Left: 'Belle' a modern hose-in-hose primrose but still quite rare
Right: jackanapes, a curious deviation from the normal primrose

plants have restarted into growth, but no buds should be apparent as yet. Disturbing the roots as little as possible, pot the plants individually into 3½ in. (9 cm) pots in a peat-based compost and press it firmly around the roots. Water well and allow to drain before placing in a shaded part of the garden.

Wait until the buds begin to open before bringing the plants into the house or conservatory, otherwise leaf growth may be excessive. Keep them in a cool place with plenty of air circulation and ample light to ensure well-balanced plants. Care will be needed with the progressively stronger sunlight and, if it is too intense through the glass, the plants may need shading. A tub may be planted with several primroses in the same way to decorate a conservatory or porch.

After flowering, they should be returned to the garden. Similarly, primroses bought as flowering pot plants early in the year may be planted outside when their flowers have finished. Providing the soil has been well prepared, they will transplant quite happily.

There are primroses of all types, sizes and colours to suit every purpose — pots, small bowls, tubs, small or large gardens. The smaller-flowered Julianas are very appealing, some with darker foliage and yet others with bicoloured flowers. Most seed lists have a wide range to offer, but for the named forms, of which there are many, it is advisable to obtain a catalogue from a reliable nursery.

17

Double primroses

I well remember my pure delight when I first saw a double primrose in flower at a specialist nursery. It was impossible to purchase one immediately and I could only place an order and wait a whole year for my plant. Considering that this happened within the last decade and was quite normal practice, it is difficult to imagine that double primroses were commonplace in the cottage gardens of old. The original double sulphur and double white were cultivated from the late sixteenth century onwards, to be joined by the double lilac and later by other colours. Despite periods of neglect, the offspring of these three predominant colours have survived throughout the intervening years and maintained their inherited vigour.

Interest in double primroses seems to have declined in the second half of the nineteenth century, only to be revived at the beginning of the twentieth. Ireland was the source of some of the choicest doubles grown then, both new and rediscovered, while others originated on the Continent. The Cocker brothers, nurserymen of Aberdeen, also developed the Bon Accord group of double primroses, in various colours and sometimes with polyanthus-type flowers. Sadly, most of these had disappeared from commerce by the 1930s. However, the few survivors have been sought out by enthusiasts and are now obtainable again.

It is always noticeable how vigorously a new seedling performs when compared with an old but precious form. Fortunately, some growers were prepared to work tirelessly to improve the double primrose, including the renowned Florence Bellis, of Oregon, USA, whose skills have presented lovers of the double primrose with an abundance of new plants in a vast range of undreamt of colours. These modern doubles have now become quite widely distributed, but it must always remain the responsibility of individual growers to ensure their continued existence.

CULTIVATION

Situation and soil

It is important to decide on the most suitable site in the garden before preparing the ground for double primroses. Partial shade and moisture-retaining soil are both essential. The shade can be provided in a variety of ways. I have grown double primroses successfully here in Kent in the dappled shade of a high fruit tree, which shields them from the hottest part of the day and prevents scorching of the leaves. However, do not plant them too close to overpowering conifers, for these retain their foliage and, without the necessary light and air, the primroses will produce too much leaf and very little flower. A northerly aspect will provide adequate light without intense glare from the sun, but be careful to avoid drying winds, which can cause distress. Protect the plants with netting, well above the foliage, if shelter from wind by other means is difficult.

The soil cannot be too rich for double primroses, for they are avid feeders. At the same time, they must have a root run that will not dry out. Plenty of peat and leafmould should be incorporated to make a friable foundation, digging them in deeply so that they are evenly distributed. Having created a suitable texture, add the food which these plants need. Composted garden waste, well-decayed animal manure and old mushroom compost should all be thoroughly dug in; the last two items can be purchased in sterilized form at most garden centres. While these elements will supply nitrogen, which is very important, potash should also be included to harden up the plants in the autumn and improve the colour and firmness of their spring flowers. Dry wood ash is the best material for the purpose, being nutritious and natural.

If the soil is largely of an acid nature, it will need toning down with a small proportion of lime. Primroses prefer an acid soil, providing it is not too excessive, but a little lime will activate any existing food in the soil. On the other hand, many new gardens contain more lime than is desirable and, if this is the case, peat should be worked in. Creating the right soil balance will make all the difference to the lifespan of double primroses.

This well-prepared soil with its friable texture and ample food supply is now ready to provide the plants with the conditions they enjoy most. I also add a small amount of bonemeal and dried blood – both slow-acting food supplements – at the recommended rate given on the containers, to ensure that the plants are never short of nourishment.

Planting, feeding and dividing

Double primroses should be planted with the same care as singles. Plant them firmly and at least 12 in. (30 cm) apart. Their roots, like those of single primroses, require coolness and moisture to thrive and throughout the growing period they should be watered frequently. However, it is their insatiable appetite for food that needs particular care. They literally exhaust themselves with the spring

Left: 'Rose o' Day', a modern double primrose
Right: 'Miss Indigo', another recently introduced double primrose which
has been achieved through micropropagation

flower display and, immediately flowering is over, they must be given a generous mulch of well-rotted animal manure and peat in order to replenish themselves. A weekly liquid feed will also help to promote new healthy growth, ensuring that fresh foliage is maintained, which in turn will keep the plants in good condition.

Double primroses are very inclined to raise themselves above soil level over a period of time, with new growth appearing higher up the rootstock. The soil should be banked up around these new roots, so that they do not lose contact with it. The doubles also need to be divided more often than their single cousins. If left undivided for more than two seasons, they will begin to die back from the centre and the whole plant may be lost. With two-year old plants, once flowering has finished, there is no time to waste. Lift the plants and gently tease the crowns apart before replanting them individually. Keep a clean sharp knife handy to trim the old leaves and roots back. This operation, repeated every other year, will enable the plants to develop their own fibrous root systems regularly.

RAISING FROM SEED

Apart from routine division, which will provide further plants, double primroses may also be increased from seed. This is available from very few firms and only a small percentage of it may result in double flowers, but it is well worth the gamble. Use the same method of sowing as for single primroses (see p.12), paying particular attention to the stragglers or later seedlings, which often produce better flowers.

Modern polyanthus

The name polyanthus comes from the Greek word *polyanthos*, meaning many flowered. Its ancestor was probably a hybrid between the primrose, *Primula vulgaris*, and the cowslip, *P. veris*, and it has characteristics of both, with one main stem arising from the crown of the plant and growing several footstalks, each bearing a single bloom. It is very variable and sometimes the solitary flowers of the primrose predominate, sometimes the umbel of the cowslip, or even one type of flower following the other.

The polyanthus was a favourite cottage garden plant from the seventeenth century onwards and many named forms were grown, although the flowers were always a reddish shade. Then, in the late nineteenth century, a chance yellow polyanthus seedling was discovered by the famous gardener, Gertrude Jekyll, and used by her as the foundation of the Munstead strain, with yellow and white flowers. The new polyanthus quickly became popular for spring bedding and commercial seedsmen were not slow to introduce their own strains, some with giant blooms and in a range of dazzling colours. Gardeners now have an enormous choice of polyanthus, including the celebrated Barnhaven strain, developed by Florence Bellis, the Pacific Giants, also from the USA, and the Cowichan strain of eyeless polyanthus.

CULTIVATION

As the polyanthus has features of the primrose and cowslip, it is no surprise to learn that it requires a method of cultivation which is a mixture of the two. With the primrose preferring dappled shade and the cowslip full sun, it is interesting that the polyanthus will thrive in a position between these two extremes. Placed a small distance from overhanging trees which have complete leaf cover only in midsummer, the plants will benefit from full sun in early spring and shade in the hotter months. Where space is limited, they may be grown in full sun permanently and will still perform satisfactorily if plenty of humus is provided around the roots. The polyanthus is vigorous by nature and should be planted in soil which has been enriched in the same way as for primroses (see p.9). The leaves grow from soil level and are designed to channel the moisture from night dews down towards the roots, which is a considerable help for the plant during long dry spells.

Polyanthus will often flower over an eight to ten week period, through April and May each year, with several stems growing from one large plant. For this reason, many gardeners plant them en masse to give a long-lasting colourful display. Ensuring sufficient moisture, particularly in summer, and giving plenty of humus and a yearly mulch are the three essential ingredients to maintain a continuous supply from your original stock of this good-tempered perennial plant.

Polyanthus multiply quickly and ideally should be divided every other year, again following the guidelines described for single primroses (see p.10). The new crowns should be replanted where they are to flower the following spring, allowing them ample time to settle in. They have a strong constitution and will die right back during winter, remaining tucked down in their winter quarters until lengthening daylight early in the year gradually reawakens them and they begin to show new spring growth. They are hardy enough to withstand long periods of deep frost, yet will still grow into vigorous healthy plants the following spring.

RAISING FROM SEED

The basic method for sowing polyanthus seed is exactly the same as for primroses (see p.12). It is important to purchase seed from a reputable source. If you cannot sow it at once, keep it in the refri-

A Barnhaven polyanthus seed strain

Left: Country Cottage mixture, an old-fashioned Barnhaven strain
Right: polyanthus Europa is a recent seed strain

gerator in the sealed packet. If you are saving your own seed, leave it to ripen before placing in a screw-top jar and storing it in the same way. The seed will rarely fail if you remember the following precautions when sowing: use seed, not potting, compost; never allow the compost to dry out; never sow when the temperature is too warm. I have always preferred to put pans of sown seed outside in the shade as previously described, for temperatures under glass can rise rapidly to a dangerous level.

Seedlings can be carefully removed from the pans after the first true leaf has developed, placing no more than 24 in each seed tray and using the same compost mixture as for primrose seedlings. The young seedlings may appear lost in the large tray at first, but if grown too closely, they would eventually become drawn as they sought sufficient light and, with less air circulation, they would be more prone to damping off. Transplanting the mature seedlings into a prepared bed in autumn is a pleasant task.

Gold-laced polyanthus

The gold-laced polyanthus, like the auricula, is still regarded as a florists' flower. It is not known how the ordinary reddish-coloured polyanthus first developed the gold or silver edging to the petals but, by the end of the eighteenth century, it had captured the imagination of florists, who concentrated their efforts into producing flowers of perfection. Their high standards are still the aim of growers today.

Although the merits of the flower may not be obvious to the beginner, its outstanding attraction is the dark ground colour – often almost black – surrounded by a fine lace edge. This lacing should be narrow and evenly distributed, not just around the edge of the petals but down the middle of each one to the central eye of the flower. The eye is all important and is most desirable when nicely rounded and bright gold in colour. The tube within the eye should display its anthers (stamens) on the same level, neither above nor below the rim. If each component were perfect, which is very rare, it would complete its wholly neat appearance.

The original gold-laced polyanthus became almost extinct by the end of the nineteenth century, but a few have been kept in cultivation by dedicated florists. In addition, modern gold-laced polyanthus have been introduced and seed and plants are available from specialists. Gold-laced polyanthus deserve to be

A gold-laced polyanthus

Double gold-laced polyanthus seed strain

highly prized and should be grown far more widely to ensure their continued existence. i have even seen them arranged as a bedding display and in a mass they were spectacular.

CULTIVATION

Gold-laced polyanthus are not difficult plants if the basic principles are followed in their cultivation, as for modern polyanthus (see p.21). Like all their primula relatives, they enjoy moisture and good food around the roots. They are completely frost-resistant and, in fact, they are much more successful in the cooler climates of the north. They thoroughly dislike a dry hot atmosphere and, when grown further south, will need adequate shading from the sun in hot dry periods. It is worth remembering that the flowers will remain darker and far more attractive with their gold edging if the plants are grown in partial shade. Watering is very important and a high potash feed in the autumn will strengthen the plants considerably before the onset of winter.

RAISING FROM SEED

Although gold-laced polyanthus may be raised from seed, the flowers of seedlings will vary. A favourite should be labelled if required for lifting and exhibiting, or purely for special attention at a later date. You will find one may be much more pleasing to the eye than another and this is the one to preserve where space is limited.

A selection of primroses and polyanthus

SINGLE PRIMROSES

Named forms

'Blue Riband'. One of the best blue primroses growing, with a vigorous and hardy constitution. The lovely blue flower is enhanced with red in its centre in spring, while the autumn flowers are more purple.

'Buckland Wine'. A compact plant bearing large wine-red flowers. This is not so easy to obtain as some single primroses.

'David Green'. The emerald green foliage sets off the deep red flowers, with only a trace of yellow in the eye, unlike many single primroses.

'Garryarde Enchantress'. A lovely plant. The flowers are cream, fused and veined with rose-pink, complemented by bronze-green leaves. 'Guinevere' also has bronzy leaves (see p.28).

Primula juliae. A compact plant with bright purple flowers and the parent of the many Julianas grown today (see pp.9 and 28).

'Queen of the Whites'. Many pure white flowers with a small yellow eye, lovely in association with the bright green foliage. A very worthwhile plant.

'Snow Cushion'. A neat plant of Dutch origin bearing tiny white flowers on short stems. One of the loveliest primroses.

Seed

Asteroid Strain. Very free-flowering and colourful. Noticeably different with orange-rust flowers showing a distinct edging.

Dania Series. Clear, bright, large flowers in a wide variety of colours. Compact plants with glossy foliage.

Europa. A new introduction particularly suited for mid-season flowering. Giant flowers on compact plants.

Juliet Mixture. Unique miniatures ideal for bowls and planters. Many are bicoloured and others have a gold lacing, combining the old-fashioned with something different.

Roggli Wonder Mixture. Now in eleven different colours, another early-flowering strain which gives a stunning display.

Spectrum Series. Outstandingly large flowers held high above the foliage in a fine mixture of colours. These have been bred particularly with the early pot plant in mind.

The colourful Wonder Mixed primroses

DOUBLE PRIMROSES

'Alba Plena'. Very free flowering, with blooms of virginal white. The original double white mentioned by the herbalist Gerard in 1597.

'Bon Accord Gem'. One of several plants raised in the early twentieth century by the Cocker brothers of Aberdeen. The flowers are bright rose shaded with mauve and it makes a very colourful plant.

'Bon Accord Lavender'. A lovely shade of lavender, with a small golden eye.

'Bon Accord Purple'. Outstandingly large, purple flowers, growing in both the primrose and polyanthus form on the same plant. This lovely plant has a strong constitution and soon grows very large (see p.28).

'Chevithorne Pink'. Evenly shaped flowers in a pretty pink. Although the plant is compact in habit, it is vigorous and long lasting.

'Crimson King'. A showy plant with flowers of a deep ruby-red on short polyanthus stems. This is one of the old forms, said to be the same as 'Old Scotch Red'.

'**Elizabeth Dickey**'. Found in Ireland in the 1930s. The flowers have the beauty and colour of the wild primrose.

'**Lilacina Plena**'. An old form thought to be a sport of *Primula vulgaris* subsp. *sibthorpii*. A beautifully formed double of purest lilac which flowers freely. It is sometimes referred to as 'Quaker's Bonnet'.

'**Marie Crousse**'. There appear to be two forms of this plant, both equally lovely. One is violet edged with white and the other splashed with white. Said to have been introduced from France over a hundred years ago.

'**Our Pat**'. A very good free-flowering double of the well-known Juliana primrose, *Primula* 'Wanda'. The flowers are purple with a sapphire sheen, complemented by foliage which has a purple tint.

'**Red Paddy**'. A neat plant of vigorous habit, with numerous blooms of cherry-red laced with silver.

POLYANTHUS

Named forms

'**Barrowby Gem**'. Although extremely rare, this is well worth seeking out. It flowers very early in the year and has a sweet almond perfume. The rich yellow flowers are shaded green, with an unusual small green eye.

'**Beamish Foam**'. An unusual dainty polyanthus with splashes of pale yellow on delicate pink flowers.

'**Duckyl's Red Cowichan**' (AM 1982). Stunning polyanthus resulting from selection over many years from the eyeless Barnhaven Cowichans, which date back to the early 1930s. The flowers have a lustre rarely seen, contrasting well with the superb dark foliage.

'**Kinlough Beauty**'. A beautiful Irish primrose of polyanthus habit. Flowers of a clear rose-pink, with a white candy stripe down each petal.

'**Lady Greer**'. A taller polyanthus-primrose with stems of 8 to 9 in. (20–23 cm), bearing many small lemon flowers above emerald green leaves.

'**McWatt's Cream**'. A beautiful compact plant with small cream flowers.

Opposite: 'Guinevere', Juliana primroses (top left and right); 'Bon Accord Purple', 'Kinlough Beauty' (centre left and right); 'Lady Greer', 'Tawny Port' (bottom left and right)

Striped flowers in the Victorians polyanthus strain

'Tawny Port'. A small plant with numerous dusky port-wine blooms over a long period. It has the added attraction of dark green leaves veined with purple and is very desirable. Originates from the west of Ireland (see p.28).

'William Genders'. A prolific plant with most unusual, white-striped, violet-pink flowers.

Seed

Crescendo F$_1$ hybrids. Typical vigour of hybrids, producing an abundance of flowers in a wide range of truly bright colours.

Giant Pacific Strain. Often grown in pots, but cool conditions are advisable to maintain the rigid stem, for they tend to grow taller than most. The flowers, in a wide variety of colours, are giant in size and excellent in form.

Gold-laced. Vigorous hardy plants, with a distinct gold lacing, though occasionally one with silver lacing is seen. They are striking with their dark mahogany grounds, sometimes even black, and well worth growing.

Silver Dollar Strain. The world-renowned Barnhaven strain contains a rich variety of delights, with such names as 'Harvest Yellow', 'Desert Sunset' and 'Spice'.

Victorians. Another outstanding Barnhaven product, the lovely blooms ranging from muted shades, through silver edged and striped to particularly bright colours.

The auricula

Introduction

Auriculas have been grown in this country for more than four hundred years. Even in the earlier part of this century, borders of auriculas were a common sight in gardens, although they are relatively rare today. Fortunately, however, auriculas are regaining popularity, not only among enthusiasts but among ordinary gardeners who have been captivated by their charms.

The ancestry of the cultivated auricula is complicated, but it is thought to derive from *Primula × pubescens*, a natural hybrid between *P. auricula* and *P. hirsuta* (*P. rubra*). These two species grow wild in the European Alps and it was from the mountainous regions of Austria that auriculas were brought into gardens, first in Vienna, then spreading across Europe and finally reaching England just before the end of the sixteenth century. There is a strong tradition that they were introduced to England by Flemish refugees, which is highly likely, since they were keen gardeners. The adaptability and toughness of this alpine plant is self-evident when we consider the different growing conditions it must have experienced on its travels.

From the simplicity of this little alpine auricula, there follows a most interesting history, which has been well documented. Its continuous cultivation and the breeding carried out over the last few centuries indicate a fascination for the plant felt by a complete cross-section of society. Soon after its arrival, it was widely grown in gardens and, by the mid-seventeenth century, there were some 40 kinds, in different colours and including double and striped forms. The latter were particularly valued and, although long since lost, double and striped auriculas are now being raised and grown again successfully.

While it remained an important garden plant, by the beginning of the eighteenth century the auricula had also become a florists' flower. These early florists formed societies throughout the country and we are indebted to them for the development of the auricula. However, the most extraordinary change in its career

31

Dusty Millers were some of the best known border auriculas

Left: 'Fleminghouse', raised in 1967, is one of the top green-edged show auriculas

Right: 'Moonlight', a strong-growing attractive self auricula
glow

took place in about 1735, when an unexpected mutation produced a green-edged flower. The peculiarly beautiful petals are leaf-like and go even further in imitation of the leaves, as they can be either lightly or heavily dusted with a powdery meal. There are no other flowers with this characteristic and to many people they appear almost unreal, even extremely delicate. At first, it was thought necessary to grow the precious new auricula in pots under cover, where it would not be blemished by rain. The edged auricula certainly looks fragile, but it is important to remember its derivation and the fact that its ancestors are immune to cold and constantly surrounded by fresh air.

The edged and other types of show auricula became the sole object of the florists' attention and enthusiasm reached its peak during the first half of the nineteenth century. After a period of neglect, the foundation of the National Auricula Society in the 1870s marked a revival of interest in auriculas, which has continued and strengthened to this day. Meanwhile, the garden or border auricula had been left to fend for itself outside, although its popularity did not decrease. Named forms ran to several hundred in the eighteenth century and Dusty Millers, so called because of their mealed foliage, could be found in many gardens. Ireland, as with primroses, was a fertile source of plants. Most of these old border auriculas have sunk into obscurity, but a small number are still available. Seed is also offered by a few specialists.

CLASSIFICATION OF AURICULAS (see also figure 3, p.36)

There are two main classes of auricula – show and alpine – and the differences between them can be defined very simply.

Show auricula

Show auriculas all share the same feature – a distinct circle of powder, like smooth chalk, in the centre of the flower, which gives it a porcelain appearance. This coating is known as paste, meal or farina and it is the way in which it develops on other parts of the flower that determines the category of show auricula (see below). Most show auriculas have mealed foliage to varying degrees as well, apart from the green-edged and some selfs.

(a) *Self.* This type has one colour only, known as the body colour, carried through from the outer rim of the central disc of paste to the edge of the flower. The body colour is velvety in texture and comes in an assortment of incredibly rich colours, from black and purple to blue, red, pink, yellow and gold.

(b) *Green-edged.* The body colour surrounding the central disc of paste is black, feathering out into pronounced green-edged petals.

(c) *Grey-edged.* The black body colour again surrounds the paste neatly, but this time feathers out into a distinctly grey edge, which is lightly covered with farina.

(d) *White-edged.* The black body colour is all the more startling in contrast to the pure white of the edge of the petals, owing to the heavy coating of farina.

(e) *Fancy.* This has the ring of paste in the centre and either a green, grey or white edge to the petals. The major distinction is the body colour, which is any colour other than black. The most

Left: 'Warwick', a grey-edged show auricula raised in the 1970s, with large flowers
Right: 'Rolt's Fancy', a green-edged fancy auricula dating from the late nineteenth century

Left: 'Phyllis Douglas', a light-centred alpine auricula dating from 1908, has proved its worth by winning a Premier Award in 1983
Right: 'Ling', a red gold-centred alpine auricula which is a strong grower

common colour is red, then yellow, and some fancy auriculas are now being developed in an attractive blue.

Alpine auricula

It should be stressed that the flowers of the alpine auricula are as large as, if not larger than, the flowers of the show auricula and that both are now equally important as florists' flowers. The word alpine is used not to indicate size but to distinguish it from the show type and the difference is unmistakable, for the whole plant is completely devoid of farina on leaves and flowers.

The centre of the flower decides into which section the alpine auricula is placed – either light-centred or gold-centred. There is no rigid shade of light or gold, but in general terms plants are described as light-centred or gold-centred alpines, with very little reference to the tremendous variation in the colour of the petals. The centre contributes much to the beauty of the flower, particularly if it is neat and round and not too large in proportion to the whole. The colours of the flowers are usually bright, either of one colour only or two-toned, with the lighter shade at the edge of the petals – reminiscent of catherine-wheels when seen collectively. The foliage is pure, fresh and green, with some leaves more rounded than others.

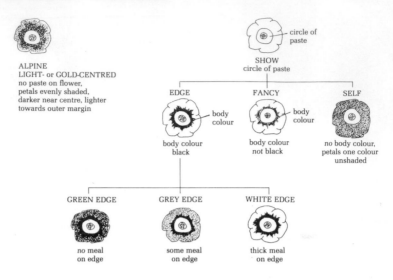

Figure 3: classification of auriculas

Outside the two main classes of show and alpine auricula are three further groups.

Double auricula

Double flowers have occurred occasionally in show and alpine auriculas, but the largest number have always been found in the border auriculas (see p.38). They vary considerably in form, some having an attractive camellia-like appearance, others having flowers frilled at the edge, with petals so numerous that the footstalks (the stalks bearing the individual flowers) need to be sturdy to support them. A new type recently developed looks almost like chiffon, in subdued chocolate and tawny colours, and has become especially sought after. The colour range is gradually widening, but at present the majority of doubles are either yellow or purple.

Striped auricula

The striped auriculas seen now are of the show type, with paste in the centre of the flower. Though a recent reintroduction, they remind us of the high value put on them when they first appeared so many years ago. The petals may be red, green, yellow or mauvy blue, each with a contrasting stripe radiating from the paste centre to the outer edge.

Above: 'Doublure', a multi-petalled double shown for the first
time in 1988
Below: 'Eadie Stripe', a modern striped auricula with old-world charm

Border auricula

The border auricula may be broadly defined as any garden auricula that does not belong to the show or alpine class. It was probably this type of auricula that was originally introduced to cultivation in the sixteenth century. The flowers have a gentle subtleness and are often lightly dusted with the farina seen on the show auricula, as well as being sweetly perfumed, while the serrated leaves may be heavily covered with meal.

Offsets of border auriculas can be taken each year (see p.49) and grown on as pot plants in the cold greenhouse or frame, in the same way as other auriculas. However, they are excellent all-year-round garden plants, being completely hardy and resilient to weather. They will form large clumps in a border and flower regularly each spring. Border auriculas need a well-drained position in a fairly humus-rich soil and dislike becoming waterlogged. They are best in dappled shade. Plants should be split every three or four years and the larger offsets replanted immediately. A top dressing to replenish them will also avoid lanky stems.

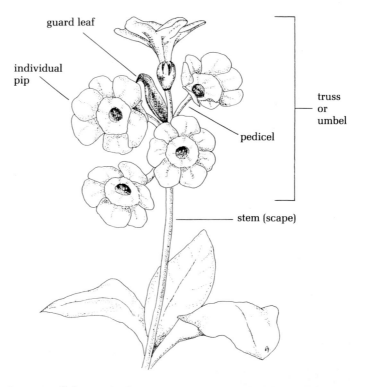

Figure 4: parts of the auricula

Cultivation of auriculas

All auriculas are hardy and will grow perfectly well in the garden, if you wish. The main reason for growing them in pots under glass is to protect the flowers from rain, particularly those of the show auriculas, whose paste can be easily spoilt. Most growers, therefore, keep them in a cold greenhouse, which must be well ventilated, or in a cold frame.

COMPOST AND POTS

Apart from the seedling stage, a loam-based compost with added ingredients is recommended for growing auriculas. The mixture has to provide for the needs of the plants for at least 12 months, including the flowering period, and if it is hastily put together, with little regard for the contents, the plants may quickly deteriorate. Sometimes their discomfort is not immediately obvious and much time can be wasted.

Using a 2 gallon (9 litre) bucket as a measure, mix the following:

2 measures JI no. 2 or sterilized loam
1 measure moss peat
$\frac{1}{2}$ measure Silvaperl or grit
$\frac{1}{4}$ measure silver sand
1 level dessertspoon each of Vitax q4 (slow-release fertilizer); charcoal (for sweetening the soil); and lime
2 oz (60 g) gamma-BHC dust (containing gamma-HCH, as a precaution against vine weevil)

Mix thoroughly, ensuring that all additives are spread evenly throughout. Silvaperl or grit completely aerates the mixture, reducing the risk of compaction, and provides ample drainage at the same time, which is extremely important; its sterility also means that it is disease-free. My auriculas thrive in this clean sweet mixture.

A $3\frac{1}{2}$ in. (9 cm) pot is ideal for most mature plants, but there may be the occasional large and vigorous plant for which a 4 in. (10 cm) pot will be necessary. I use plastic pots, but clay pots are perfectly suitable. As with all materials, cleanliness is of the utmost importance and pots should be washed in disinfectant.

GROWER'S CALENDAR

The cultural needs of the auricula are simple and easy to meet if you have a basic understanding of its manner of growth through each season. The auricula year begins as soon as flowering has finished and the following guide will help you to care for your plants successfully, mindful of the variable climate we all experience.

Early summer

Repotting usually starts in June and is the most important task once flowering is over. The plant is naturally in need of a rest and can achieve this more satisfactorily if it feels refreshed, in new compost and in a cooler situation. Repotting is also an opportunity to examine the plant thoroughly. Have a clean sharp knife ready and some sulphur dust. Push the plant out of the pot, remove the old compost carefully and hold the plant firmly just below the foliage, avoiding any damage to the new strong white roots developing directly underneath from the neck of the plant. Inspect the carrot (rootstock) and cut away any diseased parts with the knife, sealing the exposed wounds with a liberal dusting of sulphur. Pay particular attention to the lower end of the carrot, which by now has often fulfilled its usefulness and will have few if any roots growing from it. This portion may come away naturally with a little finger pressure, leaving the upper part healthy and ready for repotting. However, in some cases quite a large section of the lower carrot must be cut off, if it has gone soft or looks unhealthy, and the wound should be sealed with sulphur. Many small plantlets with roots will separate from the main plant at this stage, which can be repotted and grown on (see p.49).

Drainage is vital, so place crocks or a layer of grit at the base of the pot, followed by a small amount of compost. Hold the plant in position in the pot, spread the roots out evenly over the compost and fill up with compost, firmly but without compacting it too tightly. The newer strong roots at the top of the carrot will now have contact with the soil and will take over the main task of establishing themselves, while the remainder of the plant recuperates. The first watering after repotting is an important one, for the plant does not become instantly active. I like to use a watering can with a long narrow spout and give the plant a generous drink, allowing the excess to drain away. Another good method is to stand the pot in water until the soil is moistened throughout, then let it drain immediately.

The next step is to put the plant in a shady position. It will be a few weeks before signs of new growth become obvious, but when

'Cortina', a dark self show auricula fairly recently introduced, with an outstanding flower and contrasting foliage

this is noticed within the centre of the plant, you will know that the roots are becoming established and more active. Care must be taken not to overwater, but if the weather is very hot, spray overhead during the day – very gently over the mealy-leaved types – and give the occasional good drink at night. Once re-established, the plant should be moved to a lighter situation, for it is now safely past one of the critical stages of growth.

Midsummer

All growers are governed by the space and conditions at their disposal. If a greenhouse is the only place available, it must be shaded and even then the plants will frequently look tired and limp in hotter weather. This does not necessarily indicate lack of water: more often it is merely a sign of loss of moisture in the leaves, which can be remedied by lightly spraying them in the evening. The need for water has to be carefully watched all the time, but in extreme heat, *never* water in the middle of the day, only in the early morning or evening. Do not water unless the plant requires it. If the central rosette and outer leaves feel firm in the morning or evening, there are still enough reserves of moisture in the compost. If, on the other hand, the leaves feel limp and the weight of the pot is noticeably light, a thorough drink is necessary. Always water at well-spaced intervals rather than little and often.

If you have a cold frame available for their summer quarters, the plants will be far less adversely affected in the heat of the day. I remove the lights from the frames during hot dry spells and place net shading over the top, which gives the plants the atmosphere they prefer. Nature usually takes care of the watering and large amounts of rainwater have never harmed any plants grown here, provided there is plenty of drainage in the bottom of the pots. The plants also harden off nicely outside and, with their firmer growth, are more likely to cope with the rigours of winter. However, you should constantly check the condition of each plant. In particular, watch out for yellowing of the leaves, which may be due to waterlogging – perhaps a badly crocked pot or the fact that water cannot drain away from under the pot. Never leave an unhappy plant unattended: it only takes a few minutes to inspect it and correct any problems.

The seed pods which develop at this time of year must not be forgotten. Whether you want to save the seed and sow it (see p.48) is a personal choice, but the seed heads should always be removed at the upper end of the stem. This allows the shaft to wither, becoming brittle and harmless, and prevents any decay in the part of the plant from which the stem has grown. Sharp scissors will make a clean cut.

After repotting, the auricula is content to remain fairly inactive, enjoying a partial dormancy which coincides with the longest summer days. During this time the plant replenishes itself and regains its store of energy in preparation for the second period of growth. This is especially true of older plants, although young seedlings and small rooted cuttings will continue to grow quite rapidly, particularly if they are kept in a cool spot.

The auricula has become well adapted to our climate and it may be helpful for the beginner to realize that it has two main growing periods – spring and autumn – and two resting periods – summer and winter. The plant is much more active in the two cool seasons of the year, preferring to rest during the two seasons of extreme temperatures. This is why overwatering must be avoided, for any excess moisture lying in the pot could start to rot the roots and consequently the main carrot could be affected.

Autumn

With the onset of autumn, the growth of the plant will quicken and watering will have to be increased substantially. Do not, however, forget the maxim to water only when necessary. Remove all shading to admit as much light as possible into the greenhouse or frame. Replace the lights on the frames, but leave them open to allow the fullest air circulation. The foliage which gradually develops is shorter and thicker than the spring foliage,

Left: 'Backy', a lovely show auricula but not exhibited very often
Right: 'Coffee', a grey-edged fancy auricula with a colour combination of great appeal

in preparation for the coming winter, but just as attractive. A regular check on the plants is advisable and there will always be the odd dried leaf or flower stem to be removed. One danger, when the air circulation is insufficient, is a leaf turning mildewed. If this happens, immediately cut off every piece of damp leaf, clean any small wound on the plant and dust it with sulphur. The slightest hint of damp in the foliage, if left on the plant, will quickly travel to the centre, especially in the moister atmosphere of autumn. It is also beneficial to gently stir or rake the surface of the compost, which will aerate the soil mixture, and moss or weeds can be removed at the same time.

In any collection, it is not unusual for one plant to look sickly, even though all have been treated with the same care. The leaves may begin to feel papery and appear lifeless or dull. There could be many reasons, but whatever they may be, do *not* rewater in the hope that this is the only remedy. Completely remove the plant from the compost and examine the carrot for rot or any other defect. If this is present, cut away the offending part and seal the open wound as before. Then repot into fairly damp fresh compost. Do not water it for a few days; encourage it to fend for itself, which it will do very quickly by sending out new roots in the search for moisture and sustenance. If a plant like this is soaked immediately after repotting, it will seem to survive for a short time while the carrot is surrounded by water, but rotting will very soon follow. Unfortunately, there is sometimes no obvious cause for a sickly-looking plant, which is very puzzling. However, all

43

auriculas have their own built-in characteristics and occasionally one or other of them, usually an older form, is just a lazy plant.

In a mild autumn, large fleshy leaves may continue to grow, being misled by the unseasonal warmth. They will look attractive and healthy, but if cold weather descends suddenly, many plants will be unprepared. It is always safer for the auricula to approach winter with its winter coat on, which means the leaves should be firm and sturdy at this time of year. You can help the process by using a high potash feed in the water every 10 to 14 days, which will slow down the growth of leaves and strengthen them. This feed has the added advantage of creating a stronger flower within the nucleus of the plant, leading to an improved spring display.

Another common feature in this growth period is that plants begin to flower. A few do this regularly each autumn and there are many opinions as to the wisdom of removing the buds or leaving them. Some believe these unseasonal blooms, which are rarely typical of the spring ones, will weaken the plant, even perhaps lessening its chances of flowering the following spring, while others prefer to enjoy the bonus of autumn flowers. With exhibiting in mind, I now choose to take off the buds. I leave the stem until the buds are just above the level of the foliage, then carefully rub them out, using finger and thumb, which allows the remaining stem to wither and dry up before it is removed.

Winter

Winter invariably brings the unexpected and, although plants should now be well prepared for their second period of rest, it can be an anxious time for any grower, particularly a beginner. It would be difficult to recreate the conditions enjoyed by their alpine cousins in their wild state, but it helps to be aware of them. In mountainous areas where they grow, auriculas are protected with a layer of snow for long periods and sheltered from the icy blasts of wind that they so dislike. Within the protection of your greenhouse or cold frame, where they should if possible be kept at this time of year, several precautions are necessary. Avoid a stagnant damp atmosphere. Shelter plants from bitter cutting winds; netting will act as a shield if winds are severe, while admitting the fresh air. Never let soil in the pot remain too wet. Prevent water dripping from overhead. Some frames are made with the lid in two sections, which will need to be sealed with a plastic sheet to stop rain dripping through the central gap. If water is left to fall constantly into the central rosette, the whole plant will rot.

The second period of rest is vital to the plants and it is not a kindness to deprive them of it by using heat at any time. Dry frosts

The light-centred alpine auricula, 'Argus', is still winning awards

will not harm them in the least. With the roots just moist, the plant is barely active, yet it is gradually regaining energy for the spring with the protection of its winter coat. As the outer leaves die off, regular inspection of the plant to remove any debris is advisable. To water or not to water is the crucial question. The plants should be kept as dry as possible, but the compost must not dry out to a dust-like state. Never water during a prolonged frost. Wait for milder weather and then give them a drink in the morning, to allow time for any excess to drain away.

Further frosts will not hurt them if this routine is strictly followed through the depths of winter, for auriculas will be quite content in a suspended state of growth until well into January. Watering should continue exactly as before, into mid-February or beyond, depending on the prevailing weather conditions.

If you examine the plants regularly, it is very heartening to notice the first signs of life as a leaf begins to unfold from its tight centre. However, if a plant appears unwilling to liven up and stubbornly remains limp, it can be a sign that it has been kept too dry for too long. To avoid it becoming a complete casualty, bring it into the house, give it a generous watering and, when it starts to recover, return it to the greenhouse on one of the slightly milder days.

Late winter to early spring

You may notice that the compost appears hard and solid on the surface and a light stirring will allow air into the soil, to promote a

Left: 'Prince John', a red gold-centred alpine auricula raised by James Douglas in about 1916 and still popular
Right: the double auricula, 'Susannah', from 1972, is a welcome change to the colour range

healthier root action. Growers in the past took time and trouble top-dressing their plants, which meant removing the top inch of soil, then replacing it with fresh compost. This is another example of personal choice. Unless there is an obvious need for replenishment, I am inclined to leave the surface – after a slight stirring – completely intact, for I am wary of disturbing the new surface roots.

Regrowth now becomes particularly evident and a liquid high nitrogen feed once a week is beneficial, using a half-strength mixture. The first feed is usually given in late February or early March in the southern part of the country. However, the appearance of the plant really dictates the timing of the initial feed and, if it has not yet started into growth, wait for a week or two. Continue with the high nitrogen feed for approximately four to six weeks, watching the plant very closely at the same time. Immediately you see tiny flower buds emerging from deep within the plant, discontinue the nitrogen feed, which is no longer necessary.

All auriculas, with their individual characteristics, vary enormously in flowering times. The nitrogen feed, which promotes the growth of healthy foliage, should come to an abrupt end once the flower buds appear. The plant will now benefit from a high potash feed, which will help to encourage larger and brighter blooms. Using a half-strength mixture again, give a regular weekly liquid feed until the buds begin to show colour and then stop.

In March, growth becomes very rapid and interesting and the need for moisture will increase, according to the size of plant. A large-leaved plant will require more water than a smaller-leaved one. Constant attention to watering is time-consuming, but it is worth looking for limp thirsty plants, either gently touching the foliage or lifting the pots slightly to feel the weight. This is the safest course, for it is wrong to assume that all need a drink at the same time.

The foliage becomes extremely attractive in spring, particularly when covered with farina, as the thick winter leaves open out to reveal the younger richer leaves. Every care should be taken to maintain the quality and health of the foliage. Continuous air circulation and light are essential, but the use of shading will now have to be considered. A layer of open-gauge netting can be placed over the glass of the greenhouse, or it can be painted with shading. Remember, however, that the plants still need enough light to prevent drawn foliage and long weak stem growth. Depending on the site of the greenhouse or frame, light shading through which the plants receive dappled sunlight is the most suitable. Check for signs of rot, eliminating as before, and leave enough space between plants for good air circulation. During strong winds, move plants to a more sheltered spot temporarily, to protect the new young leaves. Keep an eye open for early greenfly and brush them off and destroy immediately. If odd roots appear above soil level, cover them with compost. Turn the plants if they seem to be growing to one side, seeking their share of light. These are all small tasks, but they will substantially improve the end result.

Spring

The flowering period, usually April and May, is an exciting time, even more so if you have never grown auriculas before. The flower spikes rise very quickly and the plants will now require much more water. Never saturate them, but keep them well supplied. Roots will begin to grow freely from the neck of the plant, designed to help the bloom perfect itself, and should be covered with a little compost. Ensure maximum air circulation always, which will encourage the stem to become sturdy enough to support the flower truss. Thicker-gauge shading may be necessary to lengthen the flowering time, as the sun can be very intense for many hours of the day. The foliage of the plant often indicates its needs, becoming limp when in distress; with the green-leaved forms, a glossy appearance will show you that the plant is healthy and comfortable. A constant awareness of their requirements as described will see the plants safely through this rewarding period, until they are ready yet again for their annual repotting.

47

Propagation of auriculas

SEED

Auricula seed does not breed true, but produces completely new plants (unlike offsets taken from a parent plant), which are also extremely vigorous and healthy. Depending on the parentage, known or unknown, the most exquisite flowers can be achieved and it is this uncertainty which spurs growers on to cross one form with another in the search for something new (see p.51).

Seed from show and alpine auriculas is never very plentiful. Seasonal conditions affect the pollen and the few pods that swell do not provide large amounts of seeds. It is important, therefore, to gain the highest germination rate possible of this precious commodity. There is a wide variety of sowing methods used by experienced growers, but I can only describe the method I have used successfully here and at the same time explain some obvious do's and don't's. It should be pointed out that the auricula is an alpine plant and the seeds do not germinate simultaneously, like those of annual bedding plants, but are notoriously inconsistent.

Collect the seed pods in midsummer just before they burst, when they are firm to the touch and beginning to turn from green to light brown. Be careful to cut high on the stem and place the pods in a strong paper bag, keeping them in this until the seed is ripe and starting to drop from the pods. Shake the bag intermittently and, when the seed has ripened completely, transfer it to an airtight container and store in the refrigerator.

The seed is sown in February using a proprietary peat-based seed compost. Fill a shallow seed pan to within 1 in. (2.5 cm) of the top with moistened compost and level it. Sow the seed evenly over the surface and cover very thinly with sand or sieved compost. This covering must be extremely fine in order not to exclude light, which is essential for germination. Spray the surface with water immediately and cover the pan with a fine net, firmly held in place under the pan. Place the pan outside, preferably on a raised shelf where it is sheltered from strong winds which might up-end it. Remember that the compost must *never* be allowed to dry out. Even one hour can be fatal, although this rarely happens when the seed pan is left outside. The best results have been obtained here following heavy falls of snow and deep frosts.

The seeds germinate erratically at varying intervals and the first batch of seedlings usually appear about eight weeks after sowing.

These will need to be transplanted after their first true leaves have grown, which are easily distinguished from the initial seed leaves. A seed tray filled with the prepared loam-based compost mixture (see p.39) will take 24 seedlings and a wide shallow 4–5 in. (10–12 cm) pot will take six seedlings. They can then remain undisturbed in the cold greenhouse until they have produced their first flower, which may appear as early as the following autumn, but is more often the following spring, by which time they will have become sturdy young plants.

The original pan will still contain ungerminated seed and should remain in a cool shaded place. If moss becomes a problem, it is wiser to transfer the young seedlings carefully to a pan of fresh compost. As a safeguard, use cheshunt compound finely sprayed at the recommended dilution rate, which will keep the surface of the compost moist and also prevent seedlings from damping off. This is only likely if there is little air circulation or if they are growing too closely together. Seedlings will continue to appear through the summer and, if you have the patience, germination can go on for three years, with new seedlings germinating when the first batch have flowered for the second time. The slower-germinating seeds often produce better flowers, which is reason enough to keep the seed pan watered and cool for such a long time.

OFFSETS

Named forms of auricula can only be reproduced by vegetative propagation – by taking offsets. There are two methods.

Method 1

When the auricula is repotted in early summer (see p.40), a number of offsets will be seen growing from the carrot, just under the main crown of the plant, and from the lower parts of the root. Each will make an individual plant for the future. Use a clean sharp knife and carefully cut the offsets from the plant, dusting all exposed surfaces with sulphur.

Larger offsets may already have roots attached, requiring gentle handling, and can be potted straight into separate 2 in. (5 cm) pots. Smaller offsets can be accommodated, three or four together, in a 3½ in. (9 cm) pot. Use the prepared moist compost mixture as before. Put the offsets around the edge of the pot, push them into the compost firmly, label and place an inverted clear glass or plastic dome on top or, failing this, a plastic bag secured just below the outer rim. Keep the pot in a cool spot out of direct sunlight. Roots will begin to develop quickly and the top growth will become noticeably sturdy when this starts to happen. Inspect the offsets every two to three days and wipe off excess moisture from inside the glass or plastic. The offsets will feel firm within 10 to 14 days and the covering should then be taken off. The rooted offsets can be safely left in the pot until the following spring and will have enough room to develop.

Some plants produce far too many offsets, crowded together just under the lower leaves of the main crown. These need to be removed carefully, whether or not extra stock is required. If they are left on the plant, the centre crown will eventually become crowded out and will be unable to gain its share of nourishment, as its new roots struggle in vain to reach the soil. Numerous offsets may also hinder the circulation of air and cause rotting.

Taking offsets is a pleasant task and one which need not be hurried. They can be taken until the end of August and the parent plant can then continue its usual pattern of growth during the rest of the year. Further offsets will develop throughout the following months and some growers, intending to exhibit their plants, remove these before spring flowering, so that all the nourishment is directed towards producing one main flower truss.

Method 2

The small, netted, peat pots known as Jiffy 7s, available from most garden centres, are used extensively here. Their merits are that they are sterile, space-saving and automatically initiate the offsets to develop rooth growth. They come in compressed form and, when immersed in water for a few minutes, swell to the size of a tiny pot ready for immediate use.

Prepare the offsets as above. If a large number are taken, a seed tray will accommodate 28 Jiffy pots; these should be allowed to drain after soaking, before the offsets are inserted. Place individual labels in each pot and press the offsets firmly into the centre, leaving approximately two thirds above soil level. Then cover with a propagating lid, to create humidity and encourage the offsets to root. Wipe off excess moisture from inside the lid regularly and examine closely for too much moisture. The new roots will soon begin to grow through the netting of the Jiffy pot, usually within 14 days, and the small plants in their pots can either be transferred to a larger tray packed with the compost mixture, or potted immediately into individual $3\frac{1}{2}$ in. (9 cm) pots. Pot them firmly with the top layer of net just above the level of the compost, which can be gradually built up as the plant develops further. Future waterings around the pot edge will ensure that excess moisture does not collect in the centre of the plant and the soil within the Jiffy pot will remain fractionally dryer, which is safer for a rootstock that dislikes damp conditions around it. The feeder roots soon forage deeply into the pot and do not appear inhibited in any way. However, if you feel that the netting might restrain them too tightly, cut a small opening through the bottom of the Jiffy pot before repotting.

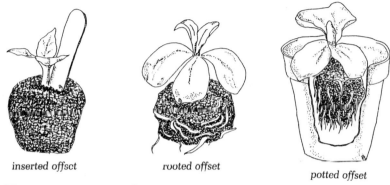

inserted offset   rooted offset

potted offset

Figure 5: propagation of auriculas, method 2

BREEDING NEW FORMS

New forms of auricula can only be raised from seed and this in itself can become a consuming hobby, as it has been for florists past and present. Many growers, as yet unacquainted with the auricula, may assume that seed from a green-edged auricula will automatically produce plants with green-edged flowers, but unfortunately this does not always happen. The genes of the new seedlings are an assortment of all that has gone before, in the same way that we may inherit a feature from a previous generation of long ago, and the progeny are likely to be inferior to the parent. For this reason, it can take many years of patient work to find an improved form, although the old florists succeeded in doing so. However, selection of both seed parents and hand pollination between them has speeded up the process and made it less unpredictable. In most cases, two good flowers of the same type are crossed (for example, a grey-edged show auricula with a grey-edged show auricula, or a light-centred alpine auricula with a light-centred alpine auricula). Named forms developed by other growers are a sound basis to work from if you wish to raise a few seedlings of your own.

The stamens or thrum of the auricula, which carry the pollen, are neatly arranged at the mouth of the tube of the flower and the

'Chloe' rivals 'Fleminghouse' in the green-edged show class

pin-shaped stigma is held below the stamens within the tube. Hand pollination can be carried out before bees or other insects get to the plants in the following way. Having chosen the mother plant, cut the top of a half-open flower just above the stigma, which is particularly sticky at this time and ready to receive the pollen from the other selected parent. The pollen is ripe immediately the flower bud opens. Use a fine camel-hair brush to apply the ripe pollen to the stigma. The egg cells soon develop and a crop of seed will ripen in just a few weeks. Label each plant bearing seed pods and note the parentage for future reference.

A selection of auriculas

SHOW AURICULAS

Selfs

'Blue Steel'. It is always interesting to see a new colour break within a range of plants. 'Blue Steel' is very appropriately named with its pale blue colouring, all other blue selfs being much darker. It created a sensation when first seen in the early 1980s and has a great future.

'Harrison Weir'. There has never been a red self to equal this one raised by James Douglas, a noted commercial grower of the nineteenth century. First shown in 1908 and has maintained its perfect form along with its vigour. It has won countless awards.

'Old Gold'. Dating back to the 1920s and always attracts attention. Its old-world charm and subtleness are irresistible. A strong-growing plant which, like many others from the Douglas nursery, has remained a favourite.

'Remus'. Raised by W. R. Hecker, an authority on auriculas, this beautiful blue self has attractively mealed leaves and bears a tall sturdy truss of flowers which are a delight to see. A strong and prolific grower.

'Rosebud'. A form from Gordon Douglas in the mid-1970s. Pink selfs are not plentiful but are in constant demand. This multiplies moderately, grows into a very strong plant and rewards the grower with its beautiful rare colouring each year.

'Sheila'. Introduced in 1961, this slightly late-flowering yellow self has won many prizes. It has a soft gentle beauty, offsets well and has continually proved to be a strong grower (see p.54).

'The Mikado'. This truly dark self has been around for many decades but never fails to delight the onlooker. Awarded a First Class Certificate in 1906 and still well worth including in a collection.

'Upton Belle'. Very large rich-coloured flowers on a strong grower. 'Upton Belle' is consistently sought after for its perfection of flower form and attractive leaf growth.

Green-edged

'Fleminghouse'. Superb in every way. It displays itself every year in all its splendour and has always remained vigorous (see p.33).

'Greenheart'. Won a Premier Award in 1967 and has remained a

Left: the yellow self, 'Sheila', introduced in 1961, can be recommended for beginners
Right: the green-edged 'Prague' grows into a very large plant and was raised in 1976

good grower. Has a fine truss of flowers every year and multiplies at a steady pace.

'Prague'. A top-class plant with outstanding form and beauty. It always looks fresh and grows vigorously. The flowers are numerous and hold themselves well above the foliage.

'Tinkerbell'. Over 50 years old, but with the help of micropropagation it is now very much rejuvenated and will readily produce a fine truss of flower. Truly outstanding when grown to perfection and, since being raised by C. Cookson in 1932, it has won many Premier Awards.

Grey/white-edged

'Lovebird'. With two Premier Awards to its credit, this auricula from James Douglas has remained an ideal collectors' plant. It is enhanced by attractive serrated leaves.

'Margaret Martin'. A consistently strong plant, award-winning and always highly desired.

'Teem'. A fine grey-edged dating from the late 1950s, which soon became one of the leading plants in its class. Many growers rely on it as a pollen parent. It is strong and healthy, inclined to be late flowering. Produces a sturdy stem with an average of 5–6 good-sized flowers each season. 'Teem' won the Corsar Cup in 1957 and has subsequently won many other awards.

'The Bride'. Raised in 1959, this is well known for its striking combination of dense paste and intense body colour. One of its

54

Left: the grey-edged 'Margaret Martin' caused a sensation when first displayed but is said to be slow to form offsets
Right: the beautiful blue light-centred alpine, 'Walton', was raised in 1957

many attractions is the slight serration of the leaves – often a sign of a superior plant.

Fancies

'Astolat'. A well-known green fancy showing an artistic refinement and perfection which can only be achieved by a florist in his prime. Raised in 1971 by W. R. Hecker, it won him a Premier Award in 1976.

'Grey Monarch'. Raised by James Douglas, this has great beauty with its wide body colour of bright gold, contrasting with the accentuated grey edge. An extremely attractive and unusual combination. It multiplies steadily and is a pleasure to grow.

'Helen Mary'. A plant which holds much promise for the adventurous grower looking for something different. With its grey-tinged green edge and blue body colour, it drew many an admirer when first shown in 1988. A new colour break which is very exciting.

'Minley'. The combination of the green edge and magenta ground colour is very appealing. It is a vigorous and multiplies rapidly.

'Rajah'. Raised by James Douglas in the 1950s, it won a Premier Award in 1978. This green-edged fancy always attracts attention, is vigorous and continues to multiply steadily.

'Redstart'. The beautiful combination of grey and red is just another example of the superb plants raised by James Douglas.

ALPINE AURICULAS

Light-centred

'Argus'. Has won many Premier Awards since it first appeared in 1897. Dark pink, has always remained vigorous and delights all who grow it (see p.45).

'Gordon Douglas'. Still a collectors' piece, which has won more awards than any other. Capable of displaying a truly remarkable truss of flowers every year, of deep violet to pale blue.

'Joy'. Raised in 1931, with rich, dark pink, unshaded flowers. 'Joy' has great beauty and perfect form, for which it has been awarded at least 13 Premiers over the years. Fortunately it multiplies readily, enabling many to enjoy this unusual alpine.

'Lady Daresbury'. Often a prizewinner and proves its worth year after year. Constantly sought after for its large, perfect, richly shaded, mauvish plum blooms. It is very strong and continues to multiply steadily.

'Walton'. Another outstanding plant from Gordon Douglas, which he considers his favourite "blue" in this class. It is strong growing and produces offsets annually (see p.55).

Gold-centred

'Janie Hill'. Introduced in 1961 and a very striking gold alpine. Received an Award of Merit and has consistently proved itself to be a most reliable grower.

DOUBLE AURICULAS

'Mary'. A pale yellow of classical form raised in 1961. It won a Premier Award in 1987. It has a strong constitution and is often used as a seed parent.

'Moonstone'. A lovely lemon double which was voted a top plant in 1987. The colour is enchanting and it has a beautiful shape. One of the more readily available doubles.

'Sarah Lodge'. First shown in 1974. There are few who can resist it, with its purplish hue and perfect shape. It has maintained its popularity since its introduction.

STRIPED AURICULAS

'Mohawk Stripe'. This is an enchanting recreation of the striped auriculas seen so long ago. It is a vigorous form which displays a fine truss of flowers every spring and will multiply at a steady rate.

Left: the double 'Moonstone' won the seedling cup in 1978
Right: 'Broadwell Gold', an excellent border auricula which was put into commerce by Joe Elliott

BORDER AURICULAS

'McWatt's Blue'. Raised by Mr McWatt, author of a book on primulas published in the 1920s, this is very eye catching, with medium-sized flowers of dark bluish mauve with a thin line of light mauve at their edge. The leaves are very heavily mealed with a slightly greyish tinge.

'Old Curiosity'. Found in a garden near Carlisle many years ago, 'Old Curiosity' is cherry red with lines of meal on its flowers and six distinct petals surrounding the white centre. The mealy leaves are inclined to become elongated. Won a Premier Award in 1985.

'Old Suffolk Bronze'. This was originally discovered by Roy Genders in a Suffolk cottage garden. It has deep plum-red, frilled flowers edged with pale ginger brown. The round centre is mealed at first but gradually fades to a golden yellow.

'Old Yellow Dusty Miller'. The Dusty Millers are the oldest surviving border auriculas and this bright yellow-flowered form is still prolific in habit. It has meal on both its flowers and leaves and remains attractive in all weathers (see p.32).

'Osborne Green'. Found in Ireland in an old cottage garden, whose owner said it had been growing there for as long as he could remember. It is most unusual with its cream-white centre and purple body colour, surrounded by a green edge, with no trace of meal.

'St Gerran's White'. A distinctive plant with light smooth leaves. It has creamy white flowers with a yellow centre, almost giving a poached egg appearance, although the yellow gradually fades as the flower ages.

Pests and diseases

Although many primroses and auriculas are grown under glass, it is vital to remember their origin and the fact that they are basically hardy plants. The hardier the plant, the stronger will be its resistance to any pest or disease. Pests will also find a plant far more succulent if soft lush growth has been encouraged by poor ventilation or overfeeding and they may introduce disease as well. The first sign of an impending problem is often apparent in the spring and fumigation at this stage is easy and effective. It will frequently eliminate trouble before it gets a hold, without damaging the plants at all. Early treatment will ensure a healthy collection of plants, but before using any pesticides or fungicides, always read the instructions carefully.

Another precaution is a matter of common sense when exchanging or purchasing plants. It is wise to isolate these newcomers until you are certain that there are no unwelcome pests dwelling undetected on the foliage or in the soil.

PESTS

Vine weevil

This pest has become the chief dread of growers of all types of pot plant in recent years and, unfortunately, this includes primroses and auriculas. It can ravage a collection in a very short time and every effort must be made to eliminate it. The adult weevil is about ⅜ in. (9 mm) long and has a short snout and hard body, which is dark grey with tiny yellow specks on the wing cases. It is nocturnal, but if disturbed during the day when at rest, it will lie completely motionless for a long period. Never be fooled into thinking it is dead, for it will eventually show signs of life and creep back to cling to the side of a pot or hide under a box until darkness. Some growers search their plants by torchlight in their determination to rid themselves of this persistent pest.

The first signs of the weevil's presence are irregular notches eaten in the leaf margins. Having fed in this way, it will then proceed to lay numerous eggs in the surface soil of the pot. These soon develop into cream-coloured legless grubs with brown heads and burrow into the soil in search of food. They feed voraciously on all root matter, which can include the entire rootstock or carrot. The larvae quickly grow into plump maggots and maintain their large appetites.

From personal experience over a number of years, I feel sure that a surface layer of grit or Silvaperl is a useful precaution and discourages the larvae from making their way down into the soil. Gamma-HCH dust already included in the compost mixture for auriculas will be a deterrent, but further measures are still advisable. Drench the pots with a product containing gamma-HCH or pirimiphos-methyl, diluted as for spraying, in early July and early August and this will help to control the newly hatched grubs.

Many growers remain unaware of the existence of this particular pest and are puzzled when a plant begins to languish for no apparent reason. Inspect any plant showing symptoms without delay, before the rosette on the surface completely collapses. If the plant has reached this stage, it may still have a stump of sorts, which can be cleaned and treated as an offset. Destroy the contents of the old pot.

Root aphid

This pest is easily recognized by its appearance, being covered with white, waxy cotton wool for its own protection. It attacks the roots, particularly those around the neck of the plant, and sucks the sap from them. If left untreated, the plant gradually becomes stunted and begins to look sickly, eventually dying.

Watering with a systemic insecticide will soon stop the pest becoming a problem if it is detected in the early stages. If it has been allowed to accumulate around the roots, remove all surrounding compost, which will be riddled with aphids, and destroy it. Make up a small quantity of systemic insecticide and pour it into a plastic dish or bucket. Immerse the plant in this solution for approximately one minute. When all the insects have died and fallen away from the roots, the plant should be repotted.

Greenfly

Greenfly and other aphids damage plants by sucking sap from the leaves, which will slowly become distorted and stunted. A greater danger is the ability of greenfly to carry virus diseases from one plant to another. It is therefore very important to combat the pest before it gets a hold and regular fumigation of the greenhouse can be extremely effective. Follow this up with the application of a systemic insecticide as required.

Red spider mite

These mites are very partial to primroses grown under glass and auriculas with mealy leaves. Under warm conditions, they spread through a collection of plants very rapidly. They are difficult to detect with the naked eye, but their presence will become obvious when the fine, pale, mottling effect is seen on the upper surface of the leaves. If untreated, the leaves will gradually become tinged around the edge, first yellow and then brown, and will completely dry out and die.

The pest can be eliminated with a systemic insecticide or pirimiphos-methyl. Even better is to take infested plants into the garden: the mites thrive in hot dry conditions, but will soon make themselves scarce when confronted with a varied climate of wind and rain. The plants will become more comfortable too, particularly when the pest leaves them alone. New growth on primroses will continue healthily and the meal on auricula leaves will develop normally.

Sciarid fly or fungus gnat

These tiny flies can be found throughout the year in greenhouses. They are attracted to peaty composts, decaying leaves and manure. They lay numerous eggs and the larvae quickly develop into minute, translucent, white maggots with shiny black heads. These are very difficult to see, but it is essential to eliminate them. They attack seedlings and offsets, burrowing directly into the stems and through into the centre of the plants, which will rot off if unprotected. However, established plants, unless damaged by other pests or overwatering, are generally not harmed by sciarid larvae.

Protect vulnerable young plants by mixing some diazinon granules with the compost. If plants do become infested, water them with pirimiphos-methyl or gamma-HCH, diluted to spray strength. Good cultivation will ensure that young plants soon grow beyond the stage at which the larvae can affect their growth.

Leafhoppers

Adult leafhoppers are $\frac{1}{12}$ in. (2–3 mm) long and are pale yellow with darker markings. Both they and their creamy white nymphs suck sap from the undersides of the leaves, resulting in a coarse pale mottling of the upper surfaces. They can be controlled as for greenfly.

Country Cottage mixed polyanthus and the Elizabethan mixture of hose-in hose

Slugs and snails

These pests can damage the leaves and flowers, both in the garden and in a greenhouse. Scatter slug pellets around the plants or spray them with a liquid slug killer.

Sparrows

Sparrows sometimes wreck primroses and polyanthus in the garden by pecking the flowers to shreds. The only certain way to prevent this is to cover the plants with netting. Less obtrusive visually is to place sticks or twigs at intervals and thread black cotton between them just above the plants.

Leaf-mining fly

Outdoor primroses and polyanthus can be attacked by a small fly that lays its eggs on the foliage. The maggots feed inside the leaves, making a white linear mine. Infestations are usually light and can be dealt with by crushing the maggot at the end of its tunnel; otherwise spray with pirimiphos-methyl or gamma-HCH.

DISEASES

Botrytis (grey mould)

With plenty of ventilation, this disease is rarely seen, but it will tend to gather where a damp or dying leaf is left on a plant. If untreated, the grey mould will develop and spread to healthy leaves and eventually into the centre of the plant, which can be fatal. It is more likely to occur late in the year in a damp atmosphere, where excess water remains on the plant. Dying leaves will then become slimy to the touch, instead of drying off and becoming brittle.

Careful removal of the leaves is a tedious job and it is easier to get every bit of wet growth with tweezers. If the dampness has travelled slightly into the centre of the plant, cut the infected part away cleanly, dust the wound with sulphur and place the plant in a position where plenty of air is freely circulating, to help its recovery. If the entire centre of the plant is affected, cut it cleanly across the top until a healthy part is left. Dust the stump with sulphur, for some side shoots will develop from eyes on the main stem and in this way the plant will not be lost. Fumigate the greenhouse with tecnazene smokes.

Soil sickness

Occasionally, a gardener may have problems with primroses which have been growing healthily in the same flower bed for many seasons. It is an unfortunate fact that soil-borne diseases can build up over a long period and the plants gradually deteriorate without obvious cause. Close inspection of the affected plants is immediately necessary. Dig up a complete plant, remove all surrounding soil and look for the following signs: a greatly reduced number of roots; rotting off at the crown; a brown core which has significantly penetrated the rootstock. Any primroses in this condition should be destroyed at once, which will probably be the majority of the plants as the disease is soil borne.

Although soil sterilants are available, they are very limited in application and, once plants have reached this sorry state, there is no cure for them and no way of killing the fungus in the soil. After the plants have been removed and disposed of, the soil in the area should not be used again for primroses or any other type of primula. The only other remedy is to take off the entire top layer of soil, to a depth of 12 to 18 in. (30–45 cm), and replace it with good fresh loam. Build this up with the addition of well-decayed manure and peat, digging thoroughly to spread the contents evenly. The newly replenished flower bed can then be used safely for primroses.

Further information

SOCIETIES

National Auricula and Primula Society
Northern Section: D. G. Hadfield (secretary), 146 Queen's Rd,
  Cheadle Hulme, Cheshire SK8 5HY
Midland and West Section: Mrs G. Baker (editor), 19 Birches Barn
  Avenue, Wolverhampton, WV3 7BT
Southern Section: L. E. Wigley (secretary), 67 Warnham Court Rd,
  Carshalton Beeches, Surrey SM5 3ND

American Primrose Society
Brian Skidmore, 6730 West Mercerway, Mercer Island, WA 98040
  USA

Dansk Primula Klub
Ove Leth-Moller, Danmarksvej 41B, 2800 Lyngby, Denmark

GARDENS TO VISIT

Broughton Castle, nr Banbury, Oxon
Chatsworth, Bakewell, Derbys
Chelsea Physic Garden, 66 Royal Hospital Rd, London SW3
Hampton Court Palace, East Molesey, Surrey
Harlow Car Gardens (Northern Horticultural Society), Harrogate,
  N Yorks
Hatfield House, Hatfield, Herts
Hyde Hall, Rettendon, nr Chelmsford, Essex
'Paddocks', Shellbrook, Ashby-de-la-Zouch, Leics
Sissinghurst Castle Garden, Sissinghurst, nr Cranbrook, Kent
Waincliffe Garden Nursery, 24 Bradford Rd, Northowram,
  Halifax, W Yorks
Wisley Garden (Royal Horticultural Society), Wisley, Nr Woking,
  Surrey

SUPPLIERS

Brenda Hyatt Auriculas, 1 Toddington Crescent, Bluebell Hill, nr
  Chatham, Kent ME5 9QT
David Chalmers, West Blackbutts, Stonehaven, Kincards AB3
  2RT

Left: 'Elsinore', a yellow self show auricula introduced in 1976
Right: 'Hermia', a light-centred alpine auricula of a most unusual palish blue

Cravens Nursery, 1 Foulds Terrace, Bingley, W Yorks BD16 4LZ

Donington Plants, Donington House, Main Rd, Wrangle, Boston, Lincs

Edrom Nurseries, Coldingham, Eyemouth, Berwicks TD14 5TZ

Hartside Nursery Garden, Low Gill House, Alston, Cumbria CA9 3BL

Holden Clough Nursery, Holden, Bolton-by-Bowland, Clitheroe, Lancs BB7 4PF

Hopleys Plants Ltd, Much Hadham, Herts SG10 6BU

W. E. Th. Ingwersen Ltd, Birch Farm Nursery, Gravetye, East Grinstead, W Sussex RH19 4LE

The Japanese Garden Co, No. 2 Home Farm, Caton, Lancaster, Lancs LA2 9NB

Martin Nest Nurseries, Grange Cottage, Harpswell Lane, Hemswell, Gainsborough, Lincs DN21 5U

Old Inn Cottage Nursery, Old Inn Cottage, Piddington, Bicester, Oxon OX6 OPY

'Paddocks', Shellbrook, Ashby-de-la-Zouch, Leics LE6 5TU (proprietor Ailsa Jackson)

Ramparts Nurseries, Hempster Farm, Berrydown, Combe Martin, Devon

F. R. Shipston, 11 Harvey Close, Allesley, Coventry, W Midlands CV5 9FU

Waincliffe Garden Nursery, 24 Bradford Rd, Northowram, Halifax, W Yorks